Edward Harold Browne

The Position and Parties of the English Church

A Pastoral Letter to the Clergy of the Diocese of Winchester

Edward Harold Browne

The Position and Parties of the English Church
A Pastoral Letter to the Clergy of the Diocese of Winchester

ISBN/EAN: 9783337760823

Printed in Europe, USA, Canada, Australia, Japan

Cover: Foto ©Lupo / pixelio.de

More available books at **www.hansebooks.com**

THE POSITION AND PARTIES OF THE ENGLISH CHURCH

A

PASTORAL LETTER

TO

THE CLERGY OF THE DIOCESE OF WINCHESTER

BY

EDWARD HAROLD

BISHOP OF WINCHESTER

SECOND EDITION

LONDON

LONGMANS, GREEN, AND CO.

1875

PASTORAL LETTER.

REVEREND BRETHREN,

I HAVE not held a visitation this year; first, because I thought that I had much to learn concerning my new and most extensive Diocese; and secondly, because I intended to have asked both clergy and laity to meet me this autumn in Diocesan Conference. I have been hindered from making this request by the rapidity with which the scheme for constituting a new Bishopric has been carried forward in Parliament. I have already said much, both in private and public, about this impending change. Let me speak very briefly of it now. I have always advocated some increase in the English Episcopate. When my eminent predecessor, Bishop Wilberforce, was taken away from us, I attended the first meeting in London for raising a monument to his memory; and I then said that I should have advocated strongly the formation of a See of South London, but that I found so many of his personal friends holding the opinion that he himself, if he had been living, would not have consented to give up that part of his jurisdiction. I knew that this was true; and so I acquiesced in a different scheme. I was not then Bishop of Winchester. No sooner was I

B

publicly named for translation than persons of weight and influence in South London communicated with me on this very subject. Earnest hopes were expressed that I would make some sacrifice to found a South London Bishopric, it being urged that no one, even of superhuman powers, could rightly administer the Diocese of Winchester, with South London at one end of it, and the Channel Islands on the coast of Normandy at the other. From that time forth I thought anxiously how I could promote this wished-for sub-division. I first proposed to give up Farnham Castle, hoping that its sale would realize a sum of money equal, or nearly equal, to the founding of a Bishopric. I was diverted from this thought, first, by being assured that Farnham would not produce nearly so large a sum as I had expected; secondly, by the thought that it was built 700 years ago by the then Bishop, Henry de Blois, brother of King Stephen, and had been the Episcopal residence ever since; and thirdly, by the unexpected discovery that property in St. James's Square had increased so greatly in value as to make Winchester House worth, perhaps, £70,000 or £80,000.

I wished originally for a Bishopric of South London only, with St. Saviour's, Southwark, as its Cathedral.[1] It would be long to tell how many different schemes were thought of and discussed in Committee and in conference with the Secretary of State, to whose

---

[1] I have still the conviction that what we want is two London dioceses; but the Thames should not be the line of demarcation. The difficulty of effecting this is very great, for it is important that the ancient See of London should embrace not only St. Paul's and the Mansion House, but Buckingham Palace and the Houses of Parliament. which form the true centre of the present metropolis.

kindness the whole Church owes much. At last it was thought that the scheme, finally brought into Parliament, though not perfect in itself, was the best that could now be devised. The result is that, when money enough is raised, South London, with its suburbs in East and Mid-Surrey, and the portion of the present Diocese of Rochester (a very small portion) now lying in Kent, will become a separate Diocese, considerable in population, but territorially very small, and so, probably, one of the most workable Dioceses in England. I cannot leave this subject without saying once more, what I have often said before, how deeply I shall feel— if I ever live to see and experience it—my separation from the portion of my present Diocese which I shall then lose. I knew little or nothing of it when I first thought of the division. I know a great deal of it now; and I have experienced so much of kindness and co-operation, both from laymen and clergymen belonging to it, that I am sometimes almost tempted to regret that I sacrificed personal friendships to public interests. But I will rather hope and pray that whatever seems privately painful may be blessed to public good.

And now let me turn from important matters, as affecting a single and more than a single Diocese, to matters still more important, as affecting the whole Church and the religious interests of millions now living and yet unborn.

We are standing, it can scarcely be doubted, on the threshold of a future history full of change in Church and State, in politics and religion. All Christendom is moved; and, strange to say, even religions outside of Christendom are moved too. It seems as if a wave of new thought and excited action were passing over the world. Men who live in such a time have much need of wisdom and self-control and disinterestedness, if they are to do their part towards making the future blessed and prosperous, instead of disastrous and evil ; and none can need these qualities so much as the clergy, who should be the pilots and directors of religious thought in a troubled sea of change and doubt. If, at similar crises in history—the Reformation, for instance —all those who thought and acted on either side had been more candid, and more temperate, and more true, there would be far less danger now, and a far brighter horizon for the future. No one can read wisely and thoughtfully the records of such times without many a pang of sorrow that men's passions checked improvements on the one hand, and marred them on the other. Are we not by such examples forewarned? and should we not be forearmed?

The Church of Christ from the earliest times has had in many ways the same elements of good and evil, so the same dangers and the same hopes as now. That Church, from its first foundation, was in one sense an absolute monarchy, because Christ is its King, and the reign of the Omnipotent must be unlimited. But, as regards its human organisation, it was so constructed as to combine order and united action with all just freedom of thought and will. If these two elements of orderly union and fair freedom had been allowed to work harmoniously together, the Church would have been, what its Founder willed it to be—a kingdom subordinate to its King and wisely regulating its citizens. But the Church had a strange struggle from the first. Its victories were its dangers. It took captive the worlds of Judaism and of heathenism and of heathen philosophy around it ; and they in their turn tried to corrupt the Christianity which had subdued them. Jews and heathens and philosophers assumed the name and profession of Christians, without renouncing either the opinions or the practices of the past. Freedom of thought ran riot, and order and unity seemed likely to be lost. When Gnostics and Ebionites and Manicheans and Arians, claiming to be Christians, were subverting Christianity, we cannot wonder that the rulers of the Church magnified, and even exaggerated, the importance of unity and order and discipline, and that, in their fears of such heresy as, in fact, meant heathenism, they should have encouraged the growth of powers inconsistent with constitutional freedom. At one time even the greatest fathers of the Church called in the strong hand of the Emperor to control the heretics ; and then, finding the sword two-edged and quite as likely to be directed against truth as against error, they turned towards another authority, which was apparently spiritual, which had never sympathised with undue license of thought, and which seemed able to unite all true believers round one common centre, and to offer a powerful resistance to the common enemy. Human wisdom could scarcely have foreseen the danger of this course. At all events, more pressing dangers were at hand. It is hard to picture to ourselves, in its full colours, the condition of Christianity in the fifth century from Christ. It had, perhaps, established itself in the convictions of the civilized world as the true religion ; but it had not interpenetrated society with its principles. The Roman Empire was not even half converted. It had followed the lead of its Emperor

and placed the cross upon the crown ; but the cruelty
and the violence and the lust and the luxury of the
Lower Empire seemed unabated, if not actually on the
increase.   The light which had streamed into it made
only the darkness visible.   Then came the Gothic tribes,
with all the fierceness of a rude race overwhelming an
effeminate civilization.   And it looked as if the Church
could only hold its own, and win its Master's way, by
forming itself into the closest possible corporation,
organising itself under a human head, and fostering
those societies of ascetic devotees, who, themselves
fighting against all the evils of a corrupt nature within,
could offer a refuge in their secluded homes from the
lust and the tyranny and the cruelty of the world
without; nay, even from the worldly conformity of the
Church itself in the profligate city and the Imperial
Court.   It is difficult now to see how all the evils of
the Middle Ages could have been encountered by Christianity if we could eliminate from history monasticism
and the Pope; and yet they appear, even in their
earliest development, excrescences upon the Church,
inconsistent with its truest principles, and naturally
productive of dangers and corruptions. He, who guides
all things, permits many things not wholly accordant
with His will, and yet guides them still—guides them to
good—until at length, through the fuller development
of evil within them, they, perhaps, become only instru-
ments of ill.   The Papacy and the monastic orders
seemed to promise security for order and orthodoxy
and Christian union.   In the end they subverted all.
Pressing to excess the claims of order, they suppressed
to excess the claims of free thought.   It was inevitable
that free thought so bound down should at length burst

its bonds; hence all those divisions of Christendom, to which the Church of Rome points as the disgrace of the Reformation, but which are in truth the fruits of the Papacy. I must apologise for seeming to write an historical essay, when I am professing to offer words of counsel and warning. I am inclined to think that a general survey of the past may help towards the solution of questions for the future.

The Papacy, even of the Middle Ages, was the extreme development of one important element of the Church of Christ—the element of unity and order. I will not linger on the many efforts to resist this extreme development, which, made from time to time by statesmen and Churchmen alike, finally culminated in what is called the Reformation. The Reformation was the consequence of a common feeling of wrong, a common yearning for freedom and truth; but it was multiform in its development. The Lutheran and the Anglican Reformations were conceived in a conservative spirit; the one assuming the attitude of protest when unable to effect reform; the other reforming without subverting the national Church, which had existed even before the nation itself. The Swiss Reformation was of a widely different character—Zwinglius throwing down all ancient landmarks and rejecting all ancient institutions; and then the genius of Calvin, building up a wholly new edifice, based on new principles and hedged in with new fences. The distinction is so important to ourselves that I dwell on it for a moment. The Lutherans desired to reform the German Church, eradicating its corruptions, but retaining its constitution. If they could have carried their princes and their bishops with them, they would probably, under the guidance of

Melanchthon, have effected a true *Reformation.* As it
was, they seceded, with the thought of remaining separate till such reformation might be possible, and, at the
same time, they put forth a solemn *Protest* against the
corruptions which they could not remove. The English was a true *Reformation.* Some may think it defec-
tive and others excessive ; but it was not secession, it
was not destruction, it was not revolution—it was reform.
It took a long time to effect. Its work went through
many reigns, beginning with Henry VIII., and certainly
not perfected till Charles II. It retained all fundamental doctrines, it respected all ancient formularies,
it changed no ancient constitution. It had the same
creeds, the same clergy, even the same services—trans-
lated and purged, but not abolished—the same Church
courts, the same Church laws. There was but one
thing which it absolutely swept away, viz. the usurped
supremacy of the Pope, and its natural consequences.
I am not asserting that the work was all well done, and
that there were no defects and no excesses—different
men will take differing views of this—I merely maintain
that this was the principle of Reformation in England.
So it was viewed by the bishops and clergy of the time,
whom we commonly call Reformers; so it was viewed and
treated by the statesmen, by the sovereigns, by the laws
of the land [1] ; so even was it viewed by the Pope him-

[1] 'It is certain that no English ruler, no English Parliament,
thought of setting up a new Church, but simply of reforming the
existing English Church. Nothing was further from the mind of
either Henry VIII. or of Elizabeth than the thought that either of
them was doing anything new. Neither of them ever thought for a
moment of establishing a new Church, or of establishing anything
at all. In their own eyes they were not establishing, but reforming ;
they were neither pulling down nor setting up, but simply putting

self, who would have tolerated the changes in faith and worship in the reign of Elizabeth, if only the Queen and people would have acknowledged his supremacy.

The Swiss Reformation, though called by the same name as the English, was essentially unlike it. It was probably a blessing to England, though it has been cast as a reproach, that there was no one great master-mind among her reforming clergy, such as Luther or Calvin. Matters, therefore, worked here more slowly and more safely. Calvin saw clearly the difficulty of the Swiss position. He was prepared for radical changes; but he was not ready to go all lengths with the rationalism of Zwinglius, and he knew that no religion could stand without close organisation and strong restraints. The organisation of the Ancient Church was not possible to him, as it was to the English. The rejection of the Papal absolutism had left the restraints of law feeble and helpless. So Calvin elaborated from his own fertile brain a new system, which was to be the substitute for and the rival of the old Catholic system, whether corrupted or reformed. He organised a great republic, binding it together by a strong republican government, and restraining—I had almost said enslaving—consciences, not by the power of the priest, not merely by a belief in the unlimited sovereignty of God, but by a blind submission to that sovereignty, though exercised so as

to rights. . . . There was no one act called "The Reformation"; the Reformation was the gradual result of a long series of acts. There was no one moment, no one Act of Parliament, when and by which a Church was "established"; still less was there any act by which one Church was "disestablished," and another Church "established" in its place.'—*Disestablishment and Disendowment*, by E. A. Freeman, D.C.L., LL.D.—a learned and interesting pamphlet.

to be apparently (though, of course, only apparently) arbitrary, tyrannical, and unjust. There can be no real question but that Calvinism, whether as a system of theology or as a system of Church government, was utterly unknown in early times. No trace of anything like it can be found in the first four centuries after Christ. In the fifth century a great thinker introduced from heathen into Christian philosophy a belief in the irrespective predestination of souls to eternal bliss or to eternal woe; but this belief in the hands of St. Augustine was subordinated to Church teaching and to Church authority. Thenceforth, indeed, Predestinarianism became popular among Christians; and men who, in modern phraseology, were among the highest Churchmen of the Middle Ages, were Augustinians of the straitest sect. Calvin made this special doctrine the foundation of his elaborate system, squared everything to fit it, and rejected everything that would not square with it. And along with it he established a system of Presbyterian government, though he himself acknowledged that he would have had bishops if it had been possible. It was a great experiment, a masterpiece of ecclesiastical policy; and to a marvellous degree it has succeeded. Doubtless, the Calvinistic 'Reformation' was a move, and a very extensive move, in the direction of free thought; but it was clear to Calvin that free thought required strong curbs and heavy restraints ; and so the system of Calvinism was, and still is, as exclusive, and in some respects as restrictive, as the system of Romanism itself. It was, probably, the rebound from its exclusiveness which caused the Socinianism and the Rationalism which first arose in Switzerland, and which still extensively prevail there.

We well know how much this system influenced earnest men in England in the reigns of Edward, Elizabeth, and the first Stuarts. It was apparently the strongest, boldest countermove to Popery. At first all (or almost all) who aimed at Reformation naturally sympathised with all the opponents of Rome. Romanism, the power of the Pope, and the rising powers of the Jesuits, constituted the common danger; and all who opposed the common danger seemed to be friends. Then the Marian exiles taking refuge among the Swiss brought back to England Swiss theology, and sowed it broadcast among the people, at a time when horror of the Marian persecutions, dread of Philip's invasions, and indignation against Papal conspiracies, had created a panic—cruel, alas, as it was timid—on the subject of Romanism. The Puritans, who owe their origin to this, well deserve our respectful remembrance. There was much that was noble and spirited in their sturdy independence; in their resistance to tyranny, whether civil or ecclesiastical; in their stern, simple habits of life and faith. But they were as intolerant as those to whom they were opposed, whether Papists or Anglicans. People had not learned at that time that it was possible to tolerate either doctrines or practices, without wholly agreeing with them. The question really was, in the reigns of Elizabeth, James I., and Charles I., whether the English Church, reformed but preserved, should continue the Church of the nation, or whether it should be rejected in favour of Puritanism (*i.e.* Calvinistic Presbyterianism) on the one hand, or Romanism on the other.

The Rebellion and the Revolution were the results of this fierce struggle. Since those great events the

English Church has had professedly within its bosom, what it had always had with less formal acknowledgment, two great schools of religious thought. They have been permitted to work side by side, not struggling for the absolute supremacy of the one to the utter extinction of the other, but acknowledged as necessary factors of the great National Church. It may be difficult to define exactly the relative positions of the two schools in all cases, for the various 'revivals' in the one direction or the other have been marked by various characteristics; but we may say generally, though not universally, that the one school has taken the side of order, the other craved for greater freedom of action; that the one has upheld Episcopal, the other has at least sympathised with Presbyterian, government; that the one has esteemed highly the Christian Sacraments, the other has laid most stress upon preaching the Word; that the one has been favourable to the higher adornment of Divine service, the other has been content with barer walls and simpler ceremonies; that the one has given more thought to the training of the young, the other has relied most on converting the adult sinner; that the one has been more devoted to pastoral labour, the other more zealous for public preaching and for foreign missions; that the one has produced nearly all our theological literature, the other has contributed chiefly to devotional and practical writings; that the one has made much of corporate life, the other has given its chief thoughts to personal religion; that the one looks back with sympathy and respect to Christian antiquity, feeling that in all its changes the Church has still had one stream of life running through its history, the other has, for the most part, shrunk from identifying the present with the former conditions of Christianity, believing that for centuries it existed only in the Bible, and could be scarcely found in the organised societies of the world ; that, once more, the one has dwelt much on repentance for sin and striving after holiness, the other has more cheered the penitent with the thought of pardon purchased and blessedness assured.

I am aware that the above does not characterise all members of either school, and that there are many other distinctions and differences which have frequently arisen ; but I believe that the two chief schools in the English Church have generally, though not universally, exhibited these distinguishing characteristics. We may have our closest sympathies with one or with the other ; but no one who thinks seriously can doubt that, when they have worked quietly together, the presence of both has been a blessing to the Church. The mistake of the sixteenth and seventeenth centuries was the determination of those in power, on whichever side they might be, that only one school should exist, or at all events should prevail, and that the other must succumb or secede. The true principle of a Church should be that union of order and free thought of which I spoke at first, permitting within all reasonable limits differences of sentiment such as must exist where men truly think at all ; not breaking unity of communion because of variety of thought or even of usage, but yet maintaining in all cases fundamental truth, and that outward order without which no human society can prevail and prosper. So permitted, variety rather contributes to strength than engenders weakness ; the variety itself stirs up, not to hatred, but to emulation in good works; and the danger of stagnation, imminent where all think exactly alike, is warded off by the watchfulness of one school over the deficiencies or excesses of the other. Unhappily, in such a state of things, stagnation is too often the only home for peace, and whenever zeal revives conflict revives with it. There are, indeed, those who say that the English Church holds within its bosom two different religions, two different faiths. Surely this is untrue. If we look back on our past history, and at the tenets and practices of both schools, there may have been, perhaps, in each of them some things to deplore, *erat quod tollere velles,* but in both of them there has been much to esteem; and though there may be at times points of important difference, surely they cannot be compared with the many points of agreement, or rather with the great fundamental agreement in the deep verities of the Christian faith. Can men be said to belong to two different religions, when both classes accept the same Scriptures as the authoritative rule of faith; both believe in the same mysterious, infinitely holy, infinitely merciful Triune God, loving Father, redeeming Saviour, sanctifying Spirit; both acknowledge the same corruption of our nature, the same redemption and restoration, through the incarnation and sacrifice of Christ; both join in the same public prayers, partake of the same appointed Sacraments; both look for the same Judgment, both believe in the same immortality, both expect the same rest in Paradise, both hope for the same home in Heaven? Differences, doubtless, exist, which zealous and sometimes designing men fan into a flame of discord; but the deep unity in those great points of common faith is infinitely greater than any differences of detail or of ceremonial can be. Is it not, then, wise and right to endure the diversity in subordinates, in thankfulness for unity in essentials? What can be hoped for from intolerance or extravagance? On each side of us, no doubt, there are two great human systems of doctrine and of discipline, gigantic efforts of human device. The Roman system was a masterpiece in its own way, built up gradually, almost imperceptibly; sometimes with entire honesty of purpose, from the hope of suppressing threatened dangers to the faith; sometimes with a strong desire in the master builders to aggrandise power and authority over the kingdoms and the consciences of men. The system of Calvin was also a masterpiece; a tower of strength built over against the fortress of the Papacy; meant to hold its own against the Papacy, and, perhaps, to destroy it. It, too, in all that was peculiar to it, was purely human; not gradually worked out in the lapse of ages, but sprung full-grown in a single generation, full-armed from a single brain. The natural result to us in the Church of England of pressing our own differences to a crisis will be to throw religious men on the one side into the arms of one human system, on the other into the arms of the opposite; systems to which we may willingly give all the credit that belongs to them, but which can never have on us the claims of our true mother, the ancient Apostolic Church of England, brought here, perhaps, by Apostles in Apostolic times; growing with our national growth; feeding year by year our national life; the source of our national greatness; the author of our national civilisation; not untinged in times past with errors which overspread all Christendom, but waking to a sense of their evil, and casting off the errors without losing historic faith or historic life.[1] Let us remember, too, that the Ultramontane Romanism of the present day is very different from the better forms of mediæval Christianity, and that we cannot recall the earnest, vigorous, severe spirit of Calvinism in its days of youth. It can be only in the most corrupt development of Romanism, and in a degenerate form of the extreme opposite, that we can find a refuge if we leave or lose the home which we have now. We need not be insensible to the desires for union, on the one hand with Continental Churches, on the other with the Nonconformist bodies at home. No holier desire can well animate Christian hearts. If I may speak of myself—and a Bishop may surely speak heart to heart with either clergy or laity of his diocese —I believe that through life I have laboured for no one thing so earnestly as for the union of the Churches of Christ. But of this I am very sure, that it will be a mistake of the most fatal character if we attempt either corporate union, or even concession tending to union, with the Churches of Roman obedience, whilst bound down to that obedience by the Vatican decrees,

---

[1] I, perhaps, appear to have overlooked the fact that there are *three* religious schools amongst us, and that the third, commonly now called the 'Broad' school, is increasing in strength. I have by no means forgotten this. I hope that there is a due place in English Churchmanship, not only for men of the old school of latitude divines, like Whichcote and Henry More, but for the modern school of enquiring thought, represented by Dr. Arnold, Professor Maurice, and others whom we may well honour and esteem. We need never check honest enquiry, so it be reverent and sincere. Still, I think what I have said in the text is true, that most *religious* men will, if driven from Anglicanism, take refuge in one of the schools I have spoken of, not in free enquiry; though many men will be driven into Scepticism, Rationalism, Pantheism, Atheism.

and before they have gone through internal reform and have obtained spiritual freedom, such as we ourselves did at the Reformation, or such as the Old Catholics are striving for now. We may hope and pray and labour for peace; but it must not be by a sacrifice of purity. On the other hand, I cannot believe in what is called an Evangelical alliance, much as I can sympathise with the spirit that gave rise to it. The very word ' alliance ' seems to indicate an acknowledgment that we do not care for ' unity.' Independent nations, which cannot possibly unite, make treaties of *alliance* ; but the Church should be *one* in Christ.¹ Let us do all we can to remove defects in our own system, and to exhibit its excellence for satisfying all spiritual wants. Let us act with all brotherly kindness to those who do not see as we see nor wholly walk with us. Let us work steadily and honestly in our own fields of labour, opening the bosom of the Church wide to receive all that will take refuge in its folds ; but let us not ignore our differences ; let us not concede that our own position is an usurped one, that we are not the ancient Church of this land, but merely one of the many sects which sprang up two centuries ago, and so, by throwing down the ancient landmarks, make all hopes of future unity impossible.²

¹ I rejoice to find in the Charge just delivered by the Bishop of Peterborough the same thoughts as my own on this subject, in almost the same words, though I need hardly say that neither of us could have seen each other's writings.

² There are points in which we are at one with the Roman Catholics, and points in which we are at one with the Nonconformist communions ; and it is most desirable to make the most of those points of contact as being so many hopes of union ; but we should do well, too, to look boldly at our points of fundamental difference.

C

And, as regards our action at home, if it be desirable that the great National Church should continue to hold within it two or three great schools of thought—which, when it ceases to hold, it will cease to be the National Church and become at best but a privileged sect—then surely two things should be borne in mind: First, we must allow each school fair latitude, fair freedom of thought and action, not readily troubled even if at times, especially in reactionary or exciting periods, any school should develope extreme partizans or extreme practices. We must remember that the wisest of men will have unwise followers, and must be fairly tolerant of unwisdom and extravagance. But, next, we must try to keep all schools, especially our own (if we belong to one) reasonably within those limits which are absolutely needful for the preservation of order and unity among members of the same body. Free thought and united action must be constantly kept in view. Only a sect can exist without freedom, and a Church will become a wilderness if it loses order.

Anglicans believe the Church to be a great human society, composed of visible elements, under an *invisible* King. Romanists believe the Church to be a great human society, composed of visible elements, under a *visible* King. Nonconformists and many foreign Protestants believe the Church not to be a visible human society at all, but an *invisible* company, known only to God, under an invisible King. Anglicans and Romanists believe in a Body ; Nonconformists believe only in a Spirit. Anglicans and Nonconformists equally acknowledge no Head but Christ. Romanists believe in an infallible head on earth. We may willingly hope that there may still be fundamental unity in faith, but there cannot be unity in work.

There has of late grown up a new distinction between England and Rome which is very significant. In olden times the controversy constantly was as to which could most truly claim antiquity in its favour. Both, of course, appealed to Scripture; but both, too, ap-

Let me venture, then, to suggest some principles which may tend to these ends. I am thankful that other warning voices besides my own[1] have lately been raised against the forming and uniting with societies for propagating the opinions of one party and prosecuting those of the opposite. Only ill can come of such unions, though good men may have lent themselves to them.

Let me speak next of the use of certain words, which by misuse become badges of party and often the sources and supports of erroneous thinking and teaching. It is, probably, familiar to all of us that the constant use of certain words of Scripture in the sense attributed to them by special schools or sects is calculated to obscure the meaning of Christian truth. Often, where the sense is itself good, it is not the sense in which a sacred writer has used it. The conventional use of words in religion and theology is to be avoided

pealed to the primitive interpretation of Scripture and the light which primitive practice shed upon Scripture. England still does this; but Cardinal Manning, the mouthpiece of Rome in this country, says that 'the appeal to antiquity is both a treason and a heresy. It is a treason because it rejects the Divine voice of this hour, and a heresy because it denies that voice to be Divine.'— (*Temporal Mission of the Holy Ghost*, p. 226.) And again : 'The appeal from the living voice of the Church to any tribunal whatsoever, human history included, is an act of private judgment and a treason, because that living voice is supreme ; and to appeal from that supreme voice is also a heresy, because that voice by Divine assistance is infallible.'—(Letter to the *Daily Telegraph*, Oct. 8, 1875, signed ' Henry Edward Card. Archbishop of Westminster.') I am greatly mistaken if Vincentius Lirinensis and the Church of his day—let alone Irenæus, Tertullian, &c.—would not have pronounced these sayings to be traitorous and heretical.

[1] See the Charge of the Bishop of Llandaff (1875), and his speech in Convocation in July 1875.

to the utmost; and Archbishop Whately justly observed that theological formularies ought never to be worded in Scriptural language, lest people, finding the words of their accustomed formularies occurring in the Scriptures, should suppose, without reflection, that the sense of the formulary was also of necessity the sense of the Scriptures.

To apply this principle to our present controversies ; it is much to be deplored that words are used, and often pressed by one party, which convey a very different significance to the ears of the other party. In a controversy which raged some quarter of a century back the two schools in the Church quarrelled over the term 'regenerate' in baptism, greatly because they attached two different meanings to it. Is not the same true now about such words as 'Real Presence,' 'Sacrifice,' 'Altar,' 'Priest'? Probably no one in the English Church, when he claims to hold the 'Real Presence' in the Eucharist, means that the consecrated bread and wine have literally become the natural Body and Blood of the Lord. Yet persons on the other side in controversy understand that this is meant ; and, indeed, language has been sometimes used as if the speaker or the writer desired to be so understood. Again, when the phrase 'Eucharistic Sacrifice' is adopted, and in relation to this the holy table is called 'altar,' and the ministering presbyter 'a priest,' there are many who simply understand by 'sacrifice' the slaying of a victim and offering the slain victim to God ; by 'altar,' the place on which the dying and bleeding victim is placed ; and by 'priest,' the person who slays the victim and then offers up the body and sprinkles the blood. There are many, again, who understand the words 'Eucharistic Sacrifice' to mean of necessity that the Sacrifice of Christ upon the Cross was but partial and insufficient, not in any way 'full, perfect, and sufficient,' unless supplemented by the sacrifice 'offered day by day continually' in the Eucharist by the priest. The unexplained use, therefore, of these phrases gives constant offence to many that hear them. Probably the word 'sacrifice' of the Holy Communion is used by many persons who do not altogether agree among themselves as to what they mean by it. The Fathers, undoubtedly, from very early times, spoke of 'offering,' and of the *sacrificium incruentum* as applicable to the Holy Eucharist; but there has been much difference of opinion as to the sense in which these terms were used; and there is, indeed, every degree of significance attributable to them—even from the simply Zwinglian commemoration of the great sacrifice up to the highest Roman belief, that the elements have been changed into the very crucified Body of Christ, and are offered afresh by the priest each time the mass is celebrated. I cannot help thinking that the rule of charity should make us careful to explain our language when we use that which may thus be misinterpreted.

There is another set of phrases which are used inaccurately, and often offensively. I mean the words 'Catholic,' 'Protestant,' 'Reformation,' and the like. As to the two last, I have already observed that the English, the Lutheran, the Swiss, and the Socinian Reformations, though called by the same name, were in truth vastly different events in history. The Lutheran was distinctly a protest against that which it was unable to remedy. Therefore, as it is well known, the Lutherans were the true Protestants; and were, till of late, exclusively called so by German historians. It may not be vitally important, but it seems to me very desirable, that, when we speak of the 'Reformation,' we should speak definitely and explicitly. The principles of the Swiss Reformation were not the principles of the Lutheran Reformation, nor were the principles of either of them the principles of the English Reformation. Much has been said about the word 'Protestant,' and it would be well if it could be confined to its original meaning ; but this has, perhaps, become well nigh impossible. Properly, neither the Swiss nor the English are Protestants. The Lutherans protested against what they could not remedy. They protested against the arbitrary conduct of their rulers, civil and ecclesiastical, who would not let them reform the religion of the land. The Calvinists, on the contrary, not only reformed but subverted the Church in Switzerland, and substituted a wholly new condition of faith and discipline in the cantons where they bore sway. They had, therefore, nothing to protest against. They had got the victory, and could not complain. In England, again, the Church and the nation, by a conjoint act, ejected the Papal domination, and 'set to rights' the religion of the land. It was not for English Churchmen, who accepted the Reformation, but for those who were attached to the Papacy, to protest then ; and protest they did, often and in good earnest, against the new learning and the reform of the faith, and the dethronement of the Pope. The true 'Protestants' in England were the Papists, not the Anglicans. Still, in modern times, the word 'Protestant' is so constantly used of those who agree to reject the authority of Rome that it is well nigh useless to attempt to restrict it to its historical sense; and, as the Lutherans acted wisely and temperately when they protested against the injustice of the Pope and the Emperor, I do not see why we should hesitate in such matters to throw in our lot with them. It may be wrong, indeed, to confound in one common name Anglicans, Scandinavians, Lutherans, Calvinists, Zwinglians, Socinians, and all the offshoots from any and all of them; but it is true that they all have this in common, that they reject the power of the Pope and the corruptions which that power has fostered and preserved. Some of them have worse errors; but they have rejected these.

But the word ' Catholic ' is of far more consequence; and it seems to me that, on every account, accuracy in the use of it ought conscientiously to be aimed at. It may be impossible to prevent writers in newspapers from applying it exclusively to members of the Church of Rome, it may be difficult to teach other people that it is not applicable equally to all Christian sects of whatever colour or creed ; but every well-educated man ought to know that such applications are historically inaccurate, and that the inaccuracy is mischievous. I need not say to you, my reverend brethren, that for many centuries in the history of the Christian faith, the name ' Catholic ' was held in the highest esteem ; that it did not convey the thought of communion with the Church of Rome, nor, on the other hand, did it embrace all who professed and called themselves Christians ; but that it designated that great body which continued steadfastly in the Apostles' doctrine and fellowship, in contradistinction to those who, by schism, or heresy, or unbelief, cut themselves off from the main body of the Church. As applied, therefore, to a Church in any nation or city or district, it meant the sound and orthodox Church there. Until the Bishop of Rome, by usurping an authority which was not his due, divided Christendom, first into East and West, and then into numberless sects and denominations, there was one great communion throughout the world, holding the same faith, governed by the same laws, partaking of the same sacraments. It was, therefore, called Catholic; whilst schisms and heresies, being local and partial, were un-Catholic. For English Churchmen, therefore, to admit that the Roman communion is the Catholic Church is distinctly to acknowledge that we ourselves are either schismatics or heretics. The Catholic Church of the land is the ancient, orthodox, Apostolic Church there. If we understand our position aright, we claim that the National English Church is that ancient Catholic, Apostolic, orthodox Church in England; and, with no feeling of disrespect either to members of a foreign communion or to those who have left the bosom of our own true mother, we ought not to concede to them the title of Catholics. It is an ancient, venerated name, to which the saints of early days attached the utmost consequence; and to use it carelessly is to be careless of our birthright.

And, again, if the ancient Church of a nation maintaining the ancient faith and order of the Apostles be the Catholic Church in that nation, then every member of that Church is a Catholic. It is a misuse of terms for a certain section of the Church to call itself the Catholic party, to speak of Catholics and Protestants as distinct elements in the same Church, to call certain practices Catholic and others Protestant. If the English Church be Catholic, its members are Catholics, and its practices are Catholic practices. No doubt some of its members will sympathise more with primitive, others more with mediæval, others more with modern, others even with heretical or schismatical principles ; but, so long as they remain members of a Catholic Church, they are Catholics, and the principles and practices of a Catholic Church are Catholic principles and practices.

I may seem to be dwelling on trifles, making too much of names and words ; but words are the great symbols of thought ; little words have often done great deeds ; and once, as we all know, the least of all letters settled the greatest controversy that ever shook the Church of Christ. Every conscientious Christian ought to watch and to protest against careless or ignorant or arrogant misuse of religious words. And few things, as I think, have more tended to aggravate our differences of late than such misuse, sometimes even than the right use rashly obtruded and unexplained.

But there are other symbols, even more conspicuous, though, perhaps, not more influential, than words, which occupy chief attention and cause greatest perplexity now. The use or disuse of special garments, the points of the compass to which the ministering presbyter may turn, threaten, as they have done before, the peace, perhaps the national existence, of the Church. I may fail to say anything which can help in this busy question ; but I would at least try to contribute some few words for peace. As I have just protested against a careless ignorant or irritating use of words, and also against their use in an unsound and unhistorical significance, so I would now protest against an exaggerated and unreal significance being attached to dresses or

ornaments or attitudes. It is true that one party has
claimed to wear special vestments and to worship in an
eastward direction, because they attach a doctrinal significance to these usages; and then the opposite party
has insisted on holding them to this principle; and so
things in themselves indifferent have become watch-
words of two hostile camps. It is certain that originally
neither an eastward position nor what are called Eucharistic vestments had any such significance at all.
The doctrine supposed to be symbolized is the doctrine
of sacrifice; but, if we go back to Jewish times, the
priest did not stand at the broad side of the Jewish altar
facing east, for the altar was four-square, having no one
side broader than the other; it was not fixed against a
wall, but stood free in the Temple. The priest may have
looked sometimes east, but if so he would have faced
the people who were worshipping westward; but he
quite as probably looked northward or southward or
westward when he offered sacrifice to the Lord. Nor
was it in his most gorgeous vestments that the High
Priest offered the great sacrifice. On the day of Atone-
ment he went in even to the most holy place, and
there sprinkled the blood of the sacrifice; but it was
specially prescribed that it should be in his humblest
guise, in the simple white dress common to all the
priesthood. The other most important sacrifice was
the Passover; for the slaying of which no priest's in-
tervention was prescribed; and though in later times
the ministry of the tribe of Levi was sought for, it was
without special dress or elaborate ceremonial. If we
look to the earlier ages of the Christian faith, it is
doubtful whether the bishop or presbyter did not more
frequently face westward than eastward; and it is most

probable that the bishops, priests, and deacons in the first five centuries wore only white. ('Si, in administratione sacrificiorum candidâ veste processerint.'—Hieron. *c. Pelag.* lib. i. c. 9.) The chasuble was, indeed, an ecclesiastical vestment as early as the sixth century, but as late as the ninth it belonged equally to all classes of clergy, including all the minor orders, and was by no means a distinctively priestly or sacrificial dress. ('Casula pertinet generaliter ad omnes clericos.'—Amalarius *De Eccles. Offic.* l. ii. c. 19. Amalarius wrote early in the ninth century.) The utmost, then, that can be said for the symbolism of the chasuble and the eastward position is that a feeling grew up in the Middle Ages in favour of them both in the ministration of Holy Communion; and that so by degrees their use as Eucharistic was adopted in the Church. It is impossible, with such a history, that they can properly or essentially have any sacramental or sacrificial significance. If, at any period, or under any circumstances, customs so growing up were thought inexpedient by the Church authorities, it could not but be lawful to discontinue and to interdict their use ; and to insist on them as essential, or to resist them as in themselves doctrinally erroneous, is inconsistent alike with reason and with charity.

And there are important practical reasons why, instead of forcing a doctrinal significance on these usages, we should try to detach them from it as much as possible. It is certain that those to whom we owe the present state of our formularies protested against the assigning importance or symbolical significance to similar acts. They even said that ceremonies, dresses, attitudes, were unimportant in themselves, and only valuable as serving to promote order and maintain unity.[1] I have reason to know that there are many, both clergy and laity, in the present day, who would like the use of a distinctive vestment at Holy Communion, not because they desire to symbolize some special doctrine, but because they look on that sacrament as the most sacred of Christian ordinances, intimately connected with their faith in the Great High Priest and His atoning sacrifice, bringing them into closest spiritual communion with Him who is the Food of their souls; and therefore they would wish peculiar honour to be attributed to the rite. In like manner, I know that there are many who would prefer the eastward position of the minister, not because they consider such position suited to a sacrificing priest, but for the same reason that the bishops in 1661 favoured it, viz. because, when we all pray to God, we should all look the same way, and rather avoid the appearance of addressing one another. At the time of Holy Communion it has generally been believed that the whole congregation pleads before God the merits of the one great Sacrifice once offered on the Cross, and therefore it has been thought that the priest should lead them in prayer, and not turn to them as in exhortation.[2] Others, again,

---

[1] See, for instances, the so-called ' Black Rubric ' at the end of the Communion Office, Canon XXX., and ' The Answer of the Bishops to the Exceptions of the Ministers.'—Cardwell, *Conferences*, pp. 335, *seq.* esp. pp. 348–351.

[2] ' MINISTER'S TURNING.—The minister's turning to the people is not most convenient throughout the whole ministration. When he speaks to them, as in Lessons, Absolution, and Benediction, it is convenient that he turn to them. When he speaks for them to God it is fit that they should all turn another way, as the ancient Church ever did, the reasons of which you may see Aug. lib. 2, *De Ser. Dom. in Monte.*'—Cardwell, *Conferences*, p. 353.

have the feeling that the eastward was the position generally observed in earlier times, that, not being necessarily superstitious, it need not have been changed, and that every continental communion of Christians (excepting only the Calvinists) uses the eastward position and some distinctive dress ; and they do not like to be dissociated in practice from all of these. Whether such persons are right or wrong, their feelings and opinions are consistent with the truest loyalty to the English Reformation, and they ought not to be forced to attach a significance to practices which they do not themselves attach to them, and which those practices do not necessarily involve.

But, above all, I deprecate the fastening a significance on insignificant rites for the following reason : if one party maintains that eastward celebration (for instance) means sacrifice, and the other party nails them down to their position, we cannot escape a most disastrous schism. It seems admitted by the highest legal authorities that the meaning of the rubrics on this latter point is yet not finally ascertained. If one party maintains that the doctrine of the Eucharistic Sacrifice is of the essence of Christianity, whilst the other holds that it is essentially anti-Christian (and, alas ! this is no exaggeration of what is said on either side) ; and if both maintain that this is symbolized by consecrating to the east, then it appears inevitable that if the final judgment decides that the eastward position is unlawful, one party must secede, and it is impossible to tell how many earnest men it will carry away with it ; if, on the contrary, the eastward position is decided to be the only legal position, then the other party must secede, unless, indeed, it can obtain a repeal of the rubric—a result

which must shake the whole fabric of the English
Church to its foundations, because it will unsettle that
principle of comprehension which has kept us together
for now two centuries and a quarter. Let us agree that
neither vestments nor attitude have in themselves any
doctrinal meaning whatever—and this is the only
common-sense view of the matter, the only view that
can be taken by reasonable men—and the result of an
adverse decision to either party will then be painful,
but cannot be destructive. Hopes may for a time be
ruined, but ' impavidos ferient ruinæ.'

I have been led on to speaking of Courts and Judgments. One difficulty in the way of settlement and
peace is the objection urged to the constitution and the
impartiality of the Courts. Judges are human, and I
am not concerned to defend them or their judgments
as perfect; but it is absolutely necessary that there
should be some mode of ascertaining the meaning of
laws which are confessedly obscure ; and I believe
it would be impossible to find a tribunal which would
be wholly free from blame and acceptable to all
men. The Prayer Book itself sends doubters and dis-
puters to the Bishop ; but extreme parties on either
side have found some excuse for refusing to abide by
the judgment either of the Bishop of any single
diocese, or of the collective voice of the English episcopate. In the case of a great National Church—a
Church which from very early days has been identified
with the nation, and the nation with it—there must be
some difficulty in deciding as to the constitution of
Courts which shall fairly represent the Church and the
nation and fairly satisfy the claims and the wants of
both. A Court composed wholly of ecclesiastics would,

probably, inspire no confidence in the laity. It is doubtful whether it would give full confidence to the clergy. Ecclesiastics might be the best informed on the significance of ecclesiastical language; but there would be a general suspicion that they were influenced by theological bias to the one side or to the other. An ecclesiastical synod, again, is a legislative, not a judicial body; and, though synods of bishops may in early times have acted as final Courts of Appeal, no body like our present Convocation has ever had such functions assigned to it, nor could it adequately discharge them. There seems no alternative but either a mixed Court of judges and bishops—such as the present Judicial Committee of Privy Council—or a lay Court, pure and simple, with, perhaps, the advice of episcopal assessors or theological experts. None of these can be perfect; but the decision of imperfect Courts is incomparably better than the anarchy of self-will. No doubt, even great lawyers are liable to misunderstand and misinterpret theological language; perhaps they have done so in certain cases already. No doubt, the ·proverbial impartiality of our judges is greatly tried when questions which involve either political or religious party come before them. No one can help having some political and some religious bias, be he who he may; [1] and, therefore, imperceptibly the most incorrupt of judges may be influenced either by preconceived opinions or by desire to prevent mischief, whether to Church or State. To say this is only to say that it is human to

---

[1] I believe that this is true even of a Jew or a Mahommedan or an atheist living in England. Religion and religious practices so affect all social questions that those who have no religion are yet under the influence of religious party.

err. But a Court must be human ; and, probably, there
are no men who will weigh words so carefully and
impartially as well-trained lawyers. Moreover, we
must remember that, as all religious questions likely to
come before the Courts involve civil rights and civil
penalties, it is impossible to remove them from the
review of the great Courts of law. Even if the Church
were disestablished, and her own internal Courts were
constituted of ecclesiastics only, every cause decided by
such ecclesiastical Courts, if it affected the property or
civil rights of individuals, must be open to appeal to
the Courts of the nation. It seems to me, therefore,
that our only wisdom is to use all constitutional means
of obtaining the best and most impartial Courts conceivable ; but not to refuse obedience to the Courts that
be, because they may have the imperfection which
adheres to all that is earthly. The two questions which
have most agitated men's minds—and which may again
come under the review of the Courts—are the Eastward
Position and the Eucharistic Vestments, of which I have
been speaking. Nothing can be more mischievous than
for one who may have to act as a judge to appear first
as a partizan or an advocate ; and as, even under the
new law, a bishop retains some of his judicial functions, I shall try to be as colourless as possible in what
I have to say ; but I should be glad to contribute what
little I may towards the fair consideration of these two
busy questions.

1. *The Eastward Position of the Celebrant.*—The
subject has been so largely discussed on all sides that
I have little to offer except in the way of friendly
criticism on what has been said by others. There is
no doubt but that many of the clergy have been thrown

into great perplexity by the supposed conflict of sentiment in the Mackonochie and the Purchas Judgments.
The Learned Judges in the former case pronounced that
the words '*standing* before the table,' applied to the
whole Prayer of Consecration, and that therefore Mr.
Mackonochie offended by kneeling. It seemed to follow
of necessity that he would have equally offended if he
had stood anywhere but ' *before the table.*' Yet the
Judges in the case of Hebbert *v.* Purchas decided that
this applied only to posture and not to position, and
that consecration must take place at the north side, or
north end, looking southward. It has not unnaturally
puzzled very learned as well as very simple brains to
reconcile these two dicta ; and a very high authority
in the law has even declared that they are irreconcile-
able. I confess that I am of that opinion myself. I
have never seen how to reconcile the *reasons* for the
two Judgments, though I can easily believe that both
Judgments may be correct. I say I can easily believe
—I do not venture to say that I am sure—for I think
the question still a tangled and difficult question ; and
I do not think that all which has been written on it
has fully solved its intricacies. There is one point,
however, to which I wish particularly to call attention,
because I understand that persons on both sides think
that it throws great light on the whole subject, and
will, perhaps, in the end unravel all its entanglements.
It is said that when the present rubric before the
Prayer of Consecration was drawn up very few holy
tables stood as they do now, viz. north and south, but
that they stood mostly in the body of the church east
and west. Hence it is thought that ' before the table '
meant both at the north side and facing south, and

D

yet at the same time facing the centre of the broad side of the table. And, curiously enough, the advocates of opposite sides, *e.g.* the Dean of Bristol, Canon Trevor, and Mr. Morton Shaw, in very able arguments, contend that this fact will decide the question in their own favour respectively. I believe that distinguished lawyers have agreed in this opinion, and I know that it has weighed with persons in very high position and of the highest intellectual eminence. I shrink from expressing strong dissent from an opinion so supported; but I have no manner of doubt that it is incorrect. I will give my reasons for saying so, and I am open to conviction if they can be shown to be unsound.

The rubric at the beginning of the Communion Service stood in 1549 as follows:—

'The priest, standing humbly afore the midst of the altar, shall say the Lord's Prayer, with this Collect.'

No one doubts that 'afore the midst of the altar' here meant in the centre of the west side facing east.

In 1552, and ever since to this day, the rubric has stood as follows:—

'The table, having at the Communion time a fair white linen cloth upon it, shall stand in the body of the church or in the chancel, where Morning Prayer and Evening Prayer be appointed to be said. And the priest, standing at the north side of the table, shall say the Lord's Prayer, with this Collect following.'[1]

The changes thus introduced were obviously these:—

First. The *name* is changed from altar to table.[2]

---

[1] In our present rubric there is added 'the people kneeling.'

[2] This, it is said, was done in consequence of the remonstrance of Hooper.

Secondly. A white cloth is to be placed upon it.

Thirdly. It is (at communion time) to stand either in the chancel or in the body of the church,[1] and is, therefore, to be moveable, not fixed to the east wall.

Fourthly. The priest, instead of standing 'afore' it, is to stand at its 'north side.'

To my mind the fact that 'afore' is changed into 'north side,' of itself proves that they are not convertible terms; but the point of chief importance to be noticed is this, that though there is a direction to place the holy table either in the chancel or in the nave (so clearly implying that it shall be moveable, like a table, not like an altar) yet neither here nor ever afterwards, by rubric, canon, or Act of Parliament, was there any injunction whatever by which the table, which had always stood north and south, should be turned round through an angle of 90° and stand east and west. If there ever was such injunction, I have overlooked it, and have tried to find it in vain. The custom was universal that the altar or table should stand with its ends to the north and south, with its longer sides to the east and west. The only effect of the Rubric of 1552,[2] and of any subsequent legal injunctions that I can find, was to make it moveable and to place it, sometimes in the chancel, sometimes (when more convenient to communicants) in the nave; but no hint is given that it should be twisted half-way round. The effect was, no

---

[1] Reading-desks had not yet obtained, and the whole service was said at the Communion-table.

[2] Let it be observed that the meaning of 'north side' in the Rubric of 1552 must rule the meaning in all subsequent rubrics, and it can hardly be contended that in 1552 holy tables had already been turned east and west.

doubt, to give it a ' table-wise ' in contradistinction to
an ' altar-wise ' position ; for it was only ' altar-wise '
according to mediæval custom when it stood at the east
end, and was fastened immoveably to the ground or to
the wall. But, I think, there can be no reasonable
doubt that in the year 1552, when first the Second
Service Book of Edward VI. came into use, all the holy
tables were standing north and south; that when they
were first removed they were simply moved forward, retaining the same position relatively to the points of the
compass ; and that if the priest stood ' afore ' the table
he could not stand at the north of it, and if he stood at the
north of it he could not stand ' afore ' it.[1] By degrees,
no doubt, and while Puritan opinions were rapidly
gaining ground through the reigns of Elizabeth, James
I., and Charles I., the holy table being removed into
the nave and the nave becoming crowded with large
pews, the custom grew up of turning the table east and
west, both to accommodate it to its place in the church,
and to make it look less and less like an altar. By degrees, probably, this altered position relatively to the
points of the compass came to be called the ' table-
wise ' in distinction to the ' altar-wise ' position ; and at
length we find the most Puritan-minded bishop of the
seventeenth century, Williams, Bishop of Lincoln, in
1627, instructing one of his clergy that the table was
to stand ' table-wise,' by which he meant east and west,

---

[1] Of course, we are all aware of the difficulty of calling the end
of a table a ' side.' I confess I see no solution of it but by admitting
that the revisers used ' side ' equally of what we now call ' ends.'
A mathematician would now speak of the four ' sides ' of a rect-
angle or other parallelogram, whether the sides were equal or un-
equal ; and the Scotch Prayer Book did undoubtedly identify north
side with north end. The holy tables in those days, too, were more
nearly square than they are now.

and the clergyman at the north *side* of it—not 'altar-wise' and the clergyman at the north *end* of it.[1] Had Bishop Williams any legal authority for saying this? Even if the Royal Commissioners who removed the altars and substituted tables for them had always placed them table-wise (and I doubt if there be proof of this), still many such acts were performed with no sufficient authority of law. It requires proof that the action and language of one arbitrary prelate is of more weight than the language of another, living at the same time, of higher rank and greater influence; and it is undoubted that Archbishop Laud, in the Scotch Prayer Book, explained north side by north end. It appears to me that there is no manner of doubt but that the meaning of the Rubric of 1552 was that, when the table was moved forward from the wall to the middle of the chancel, it should be moved as anyone would naturally move it, not altering its orientation, but carrying it simply in its original position; and that when it was moved into the nave it should be placed just before the chancel screen or chancel steps, at the east of the nave, still with the same orientation, and just as, I am told, is the custom now in many of the Lutheran churches on the Continent.

The Injunctions of Elizabeth are exactly to the same effect as the Rubric of 1552, only still more favourable to the view which I am taking. 'The holy table' is to be 'set in the place where the altar stood' . . . . 'and so to stand, saving when the Communion of the Sacrament is to be distributed; at which time the same shall be so placed in good sort within the chancel, as whereby the minister may be more conveniently heard of the communicants in his prayer and ministra-

[1] 'North side or end.'

tions, and the communicants also more conveniently
and in some number communicate with the said minister. And after the Communion is done, from time to
time the said holy table be placed where it stood
before.'[1] When the table was placed against the wall,
without doubt it stood north and south. It was moved
forward from that position farther westward in the
chancel when necessary, and then moved back to it
again. Why should the injunction mean that on every
such occasion it was not only to be moved forward,
but also to be twisted round? I am the more con-
vinced that there was no authority for this, from the
fact that of the many able and learned writers and
speakers, who maintain that the legal position was the
east and west position, not one has referred to any one
authoritative document in its favour. The only ap-
proach to authorities are the private injunction of
Williams, the great opponent of Laud, who was sure to
take the view favoured by the Puritans, and the order
of Parliament in 1640, that every Bishop should ' take
care that the communion-table in every church in his
Diocese do stand decently in the ancient *place* where
it ought to be by the law, and as it hath done the
greater part of the threescore years last past.'[2] Even
this order of Parliament says nothing, whatever it may
mean, as to the orientation of the Holy Table; and it
only speaks of the practice which it enjoins as of nearly
sixty years' prevalence, whereas the original rubric of
Edward's Second Prayer Book was nearly ninety years
older.

[1] Cardwell *Doc. Ann.* vol. i. p. 201.
[2] *Second Report of Ritual Commissioners* (556), quoted by the
Dean of Bristol, p. 27.

I maintain, then, that there neither is nor ever has been any authority for placing the table east and west, though the custom of so placing it prevailed very generally at the time when Williams tried to enforce it, and when the Laudian bishops equally tried to break through it.

When we come near to the time of the last revision, what do we find? We find, first of all, Laud, supported by the Order in Council of 1633 and the Canons of 1640 (cap. 7), trying his utmost to restore the tables to their ancient position at the east end. The Laudian prelates stood, and encouraged others to stand, at the north end, and, in the Scotch Prayer Book, explained *north side* to mean *north end.* To what extent they succeeded it is not possible to say. One difficulty they appear to have encountered, viz. that in many churches the chancels had been pulled down, though, perhaps, the chief destruction of this kind may have been done during the Commonwealth.[1] When the Rebellion came, of course, everything was upset, and the churches and services came to the hands of the revisers of 1662 in a state of chaotic confusion. But this cannot possibly be doubted, viz. that the bishops, who drew up the rubric concerning the position of the celebrant before the Prayer of Consecration, as much desired and as fully intended that the original position of the table (*i.e.* north and south, against the

---

[1] Bishop Wren says on the words of the rubric to the Communion office: ' Those words, *or in the chancel where Morning and Evening Prayer be appointed to be said,* are very ambiguous. Many churches have now no chancels; and in the most that have, though the desk for reading the prayers doth stand in the body of the church, yet they use to go into the chancel to receive the Communion.'—Bishop Jacobson's *Fragmentary Illustrations,* p. 74.

cast wall of the chancel) should be restored, as did
their predecessors, the Laudian prelates. Such a
restoration was, no doubt, but very slowly effected ;
but is it conceivable that, whereas Laud and others
had been steadily striving to restore the ancient position of the holy table, and whereas the bishops of
the reign of Charles II. (many of them having pre-
viously co-operated with Laud) equally desired that
that restoration should be carried on, yet that those
very bishops should have worded their new and most
important rubric, concerning the position of the celebrant, in such a manner that it should correspond only
with that position of the holy table which they desired to alter, which position, too, had never been given
to it by rubric, canon, or statute? Surely it was impossible. If their new rubric had been applicable only
to the east and west (or, as it had come to be called, the
' table-wise') position of the holy table, then that
rubric would have not only given new sanction to that
position, but would have fastened that position for
ever on the Church.

That the Caroline Bishops would never have done
this is infallibly certain. The history of this rubric
itself further establishes the certainty. Whatever the
rubric may mean, it undoubtedly had reference to
what had passed in the reign of Charles I. Laud and
Wren had then been accused of consecrating eastward,
with their backs to the people ; and the defence set up
was that persons of small stature could not conveniently consecrate the elements and reach the sacred
vessels from the north end of the table. Laud, no
doubt, intended that some rule should be enacted which
would provide for standing in front of the table, at

least to arrange the vessels and break the bread. The words of his MS. notes are: ' The presbyter who consecrates shall stand in the midst before the altar, that he may with the more ease and decency use both his hands, which he cannot so conveniently do standing at the north side (end) of it.'[1] And Wren's proposal for the new rubric was: ' Then the priest, standing before the table, shall so order and set the bread and wine that, while he is pronouncing the following Collect, he may readily take the bread and break it, and also take the cup, to pour into it (if he pour it not before), and then he shall say, *Almighty God, our Heavenly Father, who of thy tender mercy didst give, &c.*'[2]

There can be no doubt that these two essays at a rubric were rude draughts of that which was finally agreed on by the Caroline revisers. I do not say that the draughts and the rubric as it finally appeared necessarily enjoined the same thing; but they clearly were modifications the one of the other, and whatever was meant by the ' midst before the altar ' and ' before the table ' in these draughts was also meant by ' before the table ' in the Rubric of 1662. I conclude that in the rubrics of our present Prayer Book the north side always meant what we now call the north end, and that ' standing before the table ' meant standing on the west side of the table, between the table and the people.[3]

[1] Laud's MS. Notes, Lamb MS. 1,020, quoted by Canon Trevor, *Disputed Rubrics*, p. 72.

[2] Bishop Jacobson's *Fragmentary Illustrations*, p. 81.

[3] Since these pages have been prepared for the press, Archdeacon Harrison has kindly sent me his Charge to the Archdeaconry of Maidstone in 1875. He enters at great length into the question of the orientation of the holy table and the meaning of the words

Whether the words 'standing before the table' were intended to apply only to the time necessary for arranging the vessels, or to the saying of the whole Prayer of Consecration, is a wholly different question, and a very hard question to solve. It is possible that the revisers of 1662 may have intended to carry out the proposals of Laud and Wren, and to direct that the minister should stand before the table throughout the Prayer, and so break the bread *coram populo*, 'before the people.' It is, on the other hand, possible that they may have intended to obviate the objections which had been urged against the north-side position (viz. that it was inconvenient to reach from the north of the table to the centre), by ordering that, for the purpose of arranging the vessels, and for that purpose only, the priest should stand 'before the table,' and then return to the north end as before. It appears, however, that this is the only alternative. No third meaning can possibly have been attached to their words by those who framed this much-vexed rubric.

Men who look at the question from either extreme side appear to attach so much importance to it that those who take a moderate and middle course may well desire, when a well-defended case has been thoroughly heard and considered, that the decision may leave it open and give no triumph to either party. But I would once more earnestly plead that no one

'before the table,' and proves conclusively, though by somewhat different arguments, the very same position which I have taken in the text. One cogent argument of his is derived from the Marriage Service, where the man and the woman are to kneel ' before the Lord's table,' *i.e.* obviously betweecn the holy table and the congregation. A like conclusion is drawn from the rubric in the Coronation Service, where the Sovereign is to stand ' before the altar.'

should attach to the eastward position any doctrinal significance whatever. My own impression is, that if accidental usage had not given a bias to the two schools of thought in favour of one or other of these positions, the north-side position would be really the more suited of the two to symbolise both sacrifice and sacerdotalism. It is more likely to have been the position of the priest in the Jewish Temple; and as it turns the priest neither to the people as addressing them, nor in the same direction with them as leading them in prayer, it seems to separate him especially from them, and so to give him more the character of one belonging to a peculiar caste than any other position that could be chosen. So, surely, decency, propriety, and convenience, not deep doctrinal significance, ought to be sought for in such a case as this.

2. The '*Ornaments Rubric*' presents greater and more numerous difficulties than that which concerns the position of the celebrant; and the various judgments and interpretations have, not unnaturally, puzzled enquirers. At first sight the history seems very simple. Tho First Prayer Book of Edward VI., in the rubric before the Communion Service, ordered that the priest should wear 'a white albe, plain, with a vestment or cope.' In another rubric at the end of the whole Book it directed a surplice for ordinary services, with hoods in cathedral and collegiate churches. In this latter rubric also the bishop was enjoined at Holy Communion or 'any other public ministration,' to have 'upon him, beside his rochette, a surplice or albe and a cope or vestment, and also his pastoral staff in his hand, or else borne or holden by his chaplain.'

The Second Service Book, in 1552, swept this all

away. In this it was said, in the rubric at the beginning
of the Order for Morning and Evening Prayer: ‘And
here it is to be noted that the minister at the time of
the Communion, and at all other times of his ministration, shall use neither alb, vestment, nor cope,
but, being archbishop or bishop, he shall have and
wear a rochet; and being a priest or deacon, he shall
have and wear a surplice only.’ As the Service Book
of 1552 superseded that of 1549, so it, in its turn, was
swept away on the accession of Queen Mary. When
Elizabeth came to the throne it was debated whether
to revive the First or the Second Service Book of
Edward VI. The Queen was thought to have desired
the First; but finding this not acceptable to the feeling
of the country, then beginning to run strongly towards
Puritanism, she, and those about her, consented to
the revival of the Second Service Book, yet with certain modifications which would make it less Zwinglian.
Accordingly, in the first year of Elizabeth, 1559, an Act
of Uniformity was passed, repealing the Statute of 1st of
Mary, by which Edward's Second Service Book had been
suppressed, and enjoining the use of the said Service
Book from the Feast of the Nativity of John the Baptist,
‘ with the alterations and additions therein added and
appointed by this Statute.’ These alterations and additions are then specified; and at the end of the Act it is
added: ‘ Provided always and be it enacted, That such
ornaments of the church, and of the ministers thereof,
shall be retained and be in use as was in this Church
of England, by the authority of Parliament, in the
second year of the reign of King Edward VI., until
other order shall be taken by authority of the Queen's
Majesty, with the advice of her Commissioners ap-

pointed and authorised under the Great Seal of England for causes ecclesiastical, or of the Metropolitan of this realm.'

There can be no doubt, now, that the ornaments both of the church and the minister here referred to were those prescribed in the Prayer Book of 1549.[1] This Act, therefore, repealed the Rubric of 1552. The particular ornaments clause was, in fact, one of those ' alterations and additions added ' (to the Second Prayer Book), ' and appointed by this Statute.' [2]

It is observed that this Act does not *enjoin* the use of the ornaments of 1549, but says, ' they shall be *retained* and be *in use*.' And some have thought that the meaning of these words was that they should not be wholly swept away and forbidden, as by the Rubric of 1552, but that their retention and use should still be lawful, though not compulsory ; and this view is very consistent with the known desire of the Queen to be permitted by law to retain in her own chapels, and perhaps elsewhere also, some ceremonies and ornaments not generally accepted in the Church.[3] How-

[1] This has been repeatedly affirmed by the Supreme Court of Appeal, especially in the case Liddell *v.* Westerton.

[2] It has been said by some (*e.g.* Canon Trevor) that this Act, by reviving the second Service Book, revived its Ornament Rubric ; but as the provisional clause of the Act of Uniformity, and the subsequent rubric of Elizabeth's Prayer Book, is an entire alteration of the rubric in Edward's Second Service Book, it is not a revival but in truth a repeal of the rubric.

[3] This view of the intention of the rubric, and of the provisional clause in the Act of Uniformity, is strongly confirmed by the letter quoted (though apparently with a different intention) by the Committee of Council in the case of Hebbert *v.* Purchas. Sandys, afterwards Archbishop of York, one of the revisers of the Prayer-book, writes to Archbishop Parker : ' Our gloss upon this text is

ever, the rubric in the new Prayer Book, which was put forth immediately after the passing of this Act, and which had the Act of Parliament attached to it, not satisfied with the words ' shall be retained and be in use,' enjoined that the minister should ' *use* such ornaments, &c.'

It has been much debated whether the Queen, advised by her Council or by the Archbishop, ever modified this important clause in the Act of Uniformity, and so, too, the rubric of the Service Book of 1559. It has, at last, been ruled in the Purchas case by the Judicial Committee of Privy Council, that the Advertisements of 1564 (or, as others say, of 1566) contain that ' order taken by authority of the Queen's Majesty' which modified the rule of the Act of Uniformity and Rubric of 1559.

The words of the 'Advertisements' to this effect are as follow :—

' Item, In the administration of the Holy Communion in cathedral and collegiate churches the principal minister shall use a cope with Gospeller and Epistoler agreably : and at all other prayer to be sayde at that Communion-table to use no copes, but surplesses.

' Item, that the deane and prebendaries weare a surplesse with a silke hoode in the quyer ; and when they

---

that we shall not be forced to use them (*i.e.* the ornaments), but that others in the meantime shall not convey them away, but that they shall remain for the Queen.'—(Burnet, *Reformation*, vol. ii., Records, p. 332. See Brookes' *Privy Council Judgments*, p. 169.) This is exactly accordant with the natural meaning of the words ' shall be retained and be in use ; ' and it seems to be the interpretation of our present rubric given by the Committee of Council in Liddell *v.* Westerton. Their words are ' may be used still.'—(Brookes' *Six Judgments*, p. 53.) See below, pp. 53, 55.

preach in the cathedrall or collegiate churche to wear their hoode.'—(Cardwell, *Documentary Annals*, vol. i., p. 291.)

In another part we find the injunction : 'Archbishops and Bishops to use and continue the accustomed dress of their order.'

The Prayer Book of James I., issued in 1604, retained the Ornaments Rubric in the same form as in the Prayer Book of Elizabeth, unaffected by the Advertisements; but in the Canons, passed by Convocation in the same year, and ratified by Royal consent, the 24th Canon enjoins the use of the cope in cathedrals, ' according to the Advertisements published Anno 7 Elizabeth ' (thereby apparently recognising the authority of the said Advertisements and of the Rubric of 1559, as modified by the Advertisements); and Canon 58 enjoins, that ' every minister saying the public prayers, or ministering the Sacraments or other rites of the Church, shall wear a decent or comely surplice with sleeves, to be provided at the charge of the parish.'

There is reason to think that from that time to the Great Rebellion there was no return to the use of the albe, vestment, &c., as originally enjoined by the Prayer Book of 1549, provisionally 'retained' by the Act of Uniformity, and prescribed for use by the Prayer Book of 1559.

We come, now, to the time of the last revision in 1661–1662, which is really the turning point in the whole controversy. The great difficulty in arriving at a true interpretation of the language then used depends on a cause which was operating more or less throughout the whole of the Reformation period, viz. that there were two parties struggling for their own views and wishes; one in favour of considerable ceremony in public worship, the other earnest for the barest possible simplicity. All the way through the High Church party, however represented, would have retained something more than the surplice; all the way through the Puritan party would have swept away every ornament, whether of the church or minister, surplice and all. The Puritans, as is natural with a besieging force, directed their attacks on what they thought the weakest point, viz. the copes, vestments, &c., fully hoping to involve the surplice also in the general clean sweep of ornaments and ceremonies. The High Church party, on the other side, defended the surplice, which they felt to be the ultimate aim of Puritan onslaught, and said as little as they could about those things which they knew to be more easily exposed to popular dislike. It has been said that we ought not to attribute such tactics to Christian prelates. It may be so; but, when men so truly admirable as Baxter adopted the covert, not to say crooked, policy of the Puritans, we need not wonder that men so excellent as Sanderson and his colleagues made their moves in the like fashion of masked batteries. Neither side were willing to let the opposite party see their hands.

The Puritans evidently thought that the Ornaments Rubric of 1559, retained in 1604, notwithstanding Advertisements of Elizabeth and Canon of James I., might be held to legalise copes and vestments; and they hoped by repealing it to sweep away surplices too. In the Objections of the Ministers, it is urged, under the '18th general objection,' that significant ceremonies are not within the power of the Church authority to ordain, as they do not come under the rule of doing ‘all things decently, orderly, and to edification ; ’ and they specify the surplice, the cross in baptism, and kneeling at communion, alleging that for a hundred years these had been the fountain of evils and dissensions. When they descend to particulars and deal with particular rubrics, they say concerning the Ornaments Rubric : ‘Forasmuch as this rubrick seemeth to bring back the cope, albe, &c., and other vestments forbidden by the Common Prayer Book, 5 and 6 Edward VI., and so our reasons alleged against ceremonies under our 18th General Exception, we desire it may be wholly left out.’—(Cardwell, *Conferences*, p. 314.)

The Bishops answered the 18th General Exception (p. 345-350) by defending the right of imposing significant ceremonies, urging that it belonged to the rulers of the Church, and did not interfere with Christ’s Supreme Royalty. They then particularise for defence, as the objectors had singled out for attack, the cross, the kneeling, and the surplice ; saying, concerning the surplice : ‘ Reason and experience teach that decent ornaments and habits preserve reverence, and are held, therefore, necessary to the solemnity of royal acts, and acts of justice, and why not as well to the solemnity of religious worship ? And in particular no habit more suitable than white linen, which resembles purity and beauty, wherein angels have appeared (Rev. xv.) ; fit for those whom the Scripture calls angels ; and this habit was ancient.—Chrys. *Ho.* 60, *ad po. Antioch.*’ (Cardwell, p. 350.)

This was the Bishop’s general defence of dresses and ornaments, but especially of the surplice. When they come to the particular objection to the Ornaments

E

Rubric, they decline to enter on the question of copes, vestments, &c.; but simply refer to their general defence of ceremonies against the 18th General Exception, thus: ' 2. Rub. 2. For the reasons given in our answer to the 18th general, whither you refer us, we think it fit that the rubric continue as it is' (p. 351).

The rubric, however, did not continue as it was. It had stood unaltered from 1559, but now the revisers adopt the express words of the Statute (not of the Rubric) of 1559, omitting all allusion to modification by Royal authority, but inserting after 'ministers thereof' the words, ' at all times of their ministration.' The concluding part of the rubric, therefore, stood, and still stands, thus: 'And here it is to be noted that such ornaments of the Church and of the ministers thereof, at all times of their ministration, shall be retained and be in use as were in this Church of England by authority of Parliament in the second year of the reign of King Edward the Sixth.'

This is the whole of the history. What did it mean? Did the rubric intend to take us back simply to the Act of Uniformity of 1559, without the clause empowering the Sovereign to take fresh order for modifying it? This is certainly its most natural meaning. Did 'shall be retained and be in use' mean, ' shall be lawful but not obligatory,' as might have been its meaning in the said Act of Uniformity? or did the words mean to refer to the Act of Uniformity, as modified by the Advertisements of 1566 and by the Canons of 1604? and if so, why was no hint of such modification given? And, lastly, did ' retained' refer to the more ancient usage allowed in 1549, the second year of Edward VI., or did it only concern such remnants of those usages, if any, as had survived the various changes under Edward VI. and Mary and the gradual advance of Puritanism and the recent destruction of all habits and ornaments during the Commonwealth? These, and especially the last, are most perplexing problems. On the one hand, it is said that that cannot be *retained* which has long ceased to exist; and that, therefore, when the ornaments of 2 Edward VI. are required as to be *retained*, it must mean such as had survived till 1662 (*i.e.* only the surplice, and the cope in cathedrals). On the other hand, it is urged that 'retained,' whether in Elizabeth's Act of Uniformity or in the Rubric of 1662, could not have referred to ornaments or dresses then in actual use; for at Elizabeth's accession the dresses, &c., of 1549 had been abolished by the Second Prayer Book of Edward VI., and all post-Reformation dresses and ornaments had been superseded by the Romish or mediæval ornaments during the reign of Mary; and in 1662, on the accession of Charles II., the constant advance and ultimate success of Puritanism had swept away all the ornaments of the church and minister, whether Edwardian or Elizabethan. There was, in fact, a mere blank, a *tabula rasa*, to be filled up according to the new injunctions, whatsoever they might be. If, therefore, the rubric enjoined that only those of the Edwardian vestments which had survived all the changes were to be retained, the injunction meant nothing at all, for there was nothing to retain.

Next comes the question of contemporary exposition, the light to be thrown on the subject by usage immediately following on the enacting of a law. Great weight has naturally been attached to this. If a law

be passed of doubtful interpretation, the mode of carrying it out at the time of its enactment must be very
important in elucidating its intention. If this be conceded, it must be conceded also that, as vestments,
albes, and tunicles were not in use (or but very rarely
in use) in the reign of Charles II., the rubric could
not have been intended to enforce them. It is urged,
in reply, that the Rubric of 1662 may have been intended, not to enforce, but to permit these dresses; that
contemporaneous exposition in common law, or even,
in many cases, of ecclesiastical law, is of very different
weight from the same exposition in the case of a
rubric which had been the battle-field of a hundred
years; which itself was passed amid conflict and dissent;
which, perhaps, could only be passed in a slightly ambiguous form; which it would have been madness to
enforce, its very existence having caused the secession
of a large body of the objecting clergy and laity.

With all these difficulties, it can cause no great
wonder that there has been no great unanimity in interpreting the much-vexed rubric. Bishop Cosin, a
very eminent Caroline divine, and one of the revisers
of 1662—likely, therefore, to have understood the drift
of the rubric—is cited as holding that it enjoined
copes, vestments, &c. Bishop Phillpotts, one of the
acutest of modern expositors, pronounced the vestments legal and, under certain conditions, obligatory.
Dr. Archibald Stephens, in his learned notes to the
Prayer Book, says the same. The Judges of the Ecclesiastical Courts,[1] especially of the Court of Arches, have,
I believe, always ruled in the same direction. The
ultimate decision, of course, rests with the Queen in

[1] Dr. Lushington, Sir John Dodson, Sir R. Phillimore.

Council, and it has been thought that even the dicta of the Judicial Committee have been inconsistent and contradictory. Let us see whether this be so.

In the year 1857 a very elaborate Judgment was given (in the cases of Liddell *v.* Westerton and Liddell *v.* Beal) by a large and very learned Judicial Committee, consisting of Lord Chancellor Cranworth, Lord Wensleydale, Mr. Pemberton Leigh, Sir J. Patteson, Sir W. H. Maule, with Archbishop Sumner, and Bishop Tait. The words of the Judgment are very emphatic : ' The Rubric to the Prayer Book of Jan. 1, 1604, adopts the language of the Rubric of Elizabeth. The Rubric to the present Prayer Book adopts the language of the Statute of Elizabeth. But they all obviously mean the same thing, that the same *dresses* and the same utensils or articles which were used under the First Prayer Book of Edward VI. may be used still.' (Brookes' *Six Judgments,* p. 53.)

It was not unnatural, therefore, that thenceforth those who wished for the vestments should have considered the case to be decided in their favour ; nor was it very wonderful that the Dean of the Arches (Sir R. Phillimore) should have considered himself bound, not only by what he thought ' the plain words of the Statute,' but by the construction they had received from the Privy Council, ' to pronounce that the ornaments of the minister mentioned in the First Prayer Book of Edward VI. are those to which the present rubric referred ; ' and that ' they are, for ministers below the order of bishops, and when officiating at the Communion Service, *cope, vestment or chasuble, surplice, alb,* and *tunicle* ; in all other services the surplice only, except that in cathedral churches and colleges the academical hood may also be worn.'

This was in the case of (Elphinstone, afterwards) Hebbert *v.* Purchas. The appeal lay to the Privy Council, and the Lords who heard the appeal were Lord Chancellor Hatherley, Lord Chelmsford, Archbishop Thomson, and Bishop Jackson. The Judgment was delivered by Lord Hatherley, one of the most upright Judges that ever rose to high position at the Bar and Bench. It reversed the decision of Sir R. Phillimore, and virtually the decisions of Dr. Lushington and Sir J. Dodson. Some think that it reversed the decisions of the Judgment of the Privy Council itself in the case of Liddell *v.* Westerton, as quoted above. Was it so?

Of course, the *obiter dicta* of Judges, or the reasons which they assign for their decisions, do not form a part of their Judgment. I presume that a Judgment may hold good, and even be a good Judgment, although the reasons assigned for it may have been all unsound reasons. And on this principle we must remember that the decision in the Purchas case against the ornaments of the *minister* does not conflict with the decision in the Liddell case, which decreed that the ornaments of the *church* were those of the second year of Edward VI. It is, however, objected that the dictum of the Judges in the Liddell *v.* Westerton case was very emphatic; that it was repeated and adopted by the Committee of Council in the case of Martin *v.* Mackonochie (see Brookes, p. 127), and that it very expressly includes ' dresses,' ruling that ' the same *dresses* and the same utensils or articles which were used under the First Prayer Book of Edward VI., may still be used.' The ground on which the Judgment is based is thus accurately laid down ; and the words are very carefully chosen, apparently on the principle to which I have drawn special attention, viz. that the expression ' retained and be in use ' gave *permission* to the retention of the dresses and ornaments, rather than enforced their use : ' may still be used.' Such ruling, it is fairly contended, cannot be esteemed a mere *obiter dictum* ; it is the very ground and basis of the Judgment. Still, the Committee of Council in Hebbert *v.* Purchas has ruled that this is good of ornaments of the church, but not good of ornaments of the minister.

I presume that this ruling may be true, even though the Caroline divines intended to bring back the whole of the Rubric of 1549, and though the very learned Committee in the case of Liddell *v.* Westerton may have so interpreted their intention and have framed their Judgment accordingly ; and that for these reasons. The Caroline divines may have *intended* to make the use of the ornaments of 1549 allowable, but may have failed to word the rubric so as to *effect* their intention. Many an Act of Parliament does not make the law which its framers desired to make, even when it has been draughted by skilful lawyers. And, again, the Judges in the case of Liddell *v.* Westerton may have fully satisfied themselves that the Ornaments Rubric of 1662 re-enacted the Rubric of 1549, of which there can be no reasonable doubt ; but, not being concerned with the ornaments of the minister, but only with the ornaments of the church, they may have been satisfied to enunciate this general fact, without troubling themselves further to inquire whether that portion of the rubric which concerns the dress of the minister was

revived wholly and simply, or whether it was revived in
its modified and conditioned form. Accordingly, they
laid it down generally that the 'same dresses and the
same utensils or articles which were used under the
First Prayer Book of Edward VI. may be used still;'
but they *applied* this general rule only to the ornaments of the church. The Committee of Council, in
Hebbert *v.* Purchas, say, in effect: 'This general rule
is undoubtedly true; but the former Committee did
not enter upon the consideration of one portion of the
rubric which, in our judgment, must have been revived
in its modified, not in its original form.' The Ornament Rubrics of 1549 concern three things—the dress
of the priest, the dress of the bishop, and the ornaments of the church. Now, the Advertisements of
Elizabeth did not touch the ornaments of the church at
all; therefore, clearly, the rubrics of 1549 are revived
pure and simple as regards them. The dress of the
bishop was but slightly touched, it being only said that
bishops shall 'use and continue the accustomed dress
of their order,' whatever that may mean. But the
dress of the priest at Holy Communion, and in his
ordinary ministrations, was dealt with by the Advertisements; and so, according to the decision in the Purchas
case, the Rubric of 1549, when revived in 1662, could
only as regards the priest's dress be revived in the form
modified by the Advertisements. I should shrink from
expressing any definite opinion on these Judgments.
Questions of this kind are purely legal questions, and
eminently such as should be decided by a legal tribunal.
The intention, indeed, of those who framed the Rubric
of 1662 is at least as much a question for divines and
historians as for lawyers. An unprejudiced mind, long

familiar with the controversies and theological literature
of the sixteenth and seventeenth centuries, may be more
able to form a sound opinion on this subject than any
committee of lawyers, however learned.   I am not sure
that the very training of a legal mind does not somewhat disqualify for such enquiries.   But, as to the
legal effect of words once written down and passed into
a statute, it is obviously necessary to accept the ruling
of legal tribunals.   The tribunals which have sat
on this special rubric have fully acknowledged the
great difficulty of interpreting it ; and, as the last decision was on an undefended case, it is possible that the
question may still be revived ; but, however that may
be, we can have no hope of peace except by accepting
decisions made after full enquiry by those best qualified
to judge.   Many would have been thankful if Convocation could have initiated legislation which should
interpret the disputed rubrics so as to give no positive
victory to either of the parties which have been
struggling for ascendancy during three centuries.   On
many accounts this was impossible.   An attempt to
alter, or so to modify as virtually to alter, the Ornaments Rubric, or that concerning the position of the
celebrant, would probably have issued in a rupture
within the Church, or a rupture between Parliament
and Convocation. We can, therefore, only wait for final
interpretation and then abide by it.

    Yet we cannot be insensible to the importance of
the ultimate issue. Whenever one of the great parties in
the Church has triumphed, not by persuasion but by
legal compulsion, the Church has fearfully suffered.
The triumph of Puritanism in the time of the Commonwealth overthrew the Church.   The triumph of the

High Church party at the Restoration turned Noncon-formists into Dissenters. Soon after came the secession of the Non-jurors. Each one of these left the Church weaker against its enemies without, with less of life and energy and holiness within. At present, scarcely any de-cision can be arrived at, which will not be a severe blow to one or other of the extreme parties, and a distress to many more moderate and more reasonable men. It is quite possible to anticipate a decision which may greatly trouble all. It is certainly conceivable that, when the questions have been thoroughly discussed and counsel fully heard on every side, the final judgment may be that the vestments are legal and the eastward position illegal. Is there anybody whom this would not wound, except, indeed, those who are determined to attach no importance, doctrinally or otherwise, to attitudes and dresses? High Churchmen would be pained at finding the position, which they believe to be primitive and well-nigh universal, forbidden and proscribed; Low Churchmen would be scandalized by the sanction given to vestments which they have been used to identify with the worst errors of Rome.

Is it too late to reconsider our position and mode-rate our passions? We are in imminent danger of a rupture as great as those of the seventeenth century, but with much less reason for it.

With much less reason for it. Without question, on both sides there are a few men of extreme opinions and extreme practices; but, from the experience derived from acquaintance with two very different dioceses, I can say with confidence that the great body of the clergy are more sober and moderate in their views, and have really more sympathy with one another, than in almost any period of our past history—certainly, than in any period of active life and zeal. The so-called Evangelical clergy are, in general, far more attached and intelligent Churchmen than those of a past generation, and in this respect quite unlike the Puritans of the seventeenth century. The High Church clergy are incomparably more agreed with their Evangelical brethren on many points of faith and practice than the High Churchmen in the period of the Stuarts. Evangelicals are anxious for decency and order and even beauty of Church ornament and service, and ready to obey Church authority. High Churchmen have none of that Pelagian element in their theology, from the charge of which so great a teacher as Jeremie Taylor was not exempted. If you listen to many a High Church teacher now on the doctrine of human sin or of the atoning sacrifice of Christ, you would say that there was nothing to choose between his teaching and that of William Wilberforce or Henry Venn or Charles Simeon, except that it was somewhat more practically pointed—like Baxter rather than Romaine. Can there be no peace between such as these? And let us remember that a disruption will not rest with a few extreme men only. It will shake the building like a house of cards; you cannot tell which next will fall.

And, again, is there so much to complain of? Is it not true that each school in its turn has gained a victory? The one school could not have desired more latitude than was allowed it by the Gorham Judgment. The doctrine of the English Reformation could scarcely have been more emphatically denied than it was by Mr. Gorham. The opposite school has had as great a victory in the acquittal of Mr. Bennett for

language as strong on the Eucharist as Mr. Gorham's
was in the other direction on Holy Baptism. The
Broad Churchmen have been acquitted in the persons
of Dr. Williams and Mr. Wilson, and can have no right
to complain of persecution or intolerance. Without
question, the decisions have been more stringent in
matters of ceremonial; but that, perhaps, is not unnatural. It is easier in general to weigh a rubric than
to interpret an article of faith. It is said to be the
legal heresy, that men may think and even speak as
they list, but that they must worship in fetters. For
my own part I should like to see fair liberty of prophe-
sying, within the lawful limits of the primitive faith,
and fair freedom of worship so far as is consistent with
freedom to people as well as priests; but I do think that
the distinction is true as between preaching and ministering. A clergyman in teaching must be allowed to
speak his own thoughts and convictions, or he stammers
in a foreign tongue. No one is forced to follow all he
says, if his sayings seem unfounded in Scripture and inconsistent with the doctrines of the faith. A clergyman
ministering ministers as the Coryphæus, the fugleman,
the leader of the people. He speaks, not to them, but
for them. He acts as their leader and mouthpiece.
It must be painful to a parish if the words or the
actions of their presbyter in prayer be foreign to their
feelings and convictions. And a layman must join in
the *services* of the Church, or be a dissentient and
seceder. Hence, there seems a natural reason why the
ceremonial service of the Church should be somewhat
more strictly guarded from the idiosyncracy of the
minister than his utterances from the pulpit or in the
parish and the school. Every clergyman, indeed, has a

full right to all the freedom which the Church allows
him in prayer as much as in preaching ; but in the one
case it is more naturally restricted than in the other.
Even in things lawful I doubt if one man ought to
change forms of service and worship, till he can carry
a willing people with him ; and by people I mean
parish, not congregation only.

I have dwelt at excessive length on all these points.
I can but recur to that with which I began, pleading
for patience, endurance, and charity. Surely reasonable
men on either side will acknowledge the debt which is
due to the opposite side. I believe that every wise
man on the High Church side will feel how deep is our
obligation to those who, when a spirit of slumber and
worldly forgetfulness had so crept over the land that
it was hard to distinguish Christian theology from
Deistical indifference, raised the standard of faith in
Christ crucified and won back the wanderers to the
fresh pastures of the Gospel of God. The Evangelicals
will, surely, not deny that in all periods of our history
those High Churchmen, who have been from time to
time suspected and accused of sympathy with Romanism, have not only been the great thinkers and writers
in theology and Christian faith—such as Hooker and
Pearson and Butler and Bull and Waterland—but
have left us the strongest and most enduring defences
of the Reformed faith against the assaults of Roman and Jesuit error. Let me name Hooker,
Andrewes, Ussher, Bramhall, Jeremie Taylor, Cosin,
Sanderson, Hammond, Leslie, Bull, Beveridge, Bar-
row, Stillingfleet, Wake, even Laud himself. There
have been no more successful combatants on the
side of the Reformation anywhere ; in England they

stand quite alone ; but they were all writers of the so-called High Church school of belief.[1] Yet, with all these reasons for union, we hear from one extreme party threats of a large secession unless their voices prevail; whilst from the other we have threats of throwing themselves into the cry for disestablishment. It would be well if both would reflect that a large secession would involve disestablishment, and that conversely disestablishment would carry with it disruption. A bishop is supposed to dread disestablishment, because it would be likely to reduce his social position and to diminish his wealth. I do not on this account dread it in the least. I believe that no one would really gain by disestablishment so much as a Bishop. If my feelings were only for the aggrandisement of my order, I should work for disestablishment to-morrow. I do, indeed, deprecate disestablishment, but for very different reasons. Disestablishment would be a revolution of so extensive a nature that it could not but carry other revolutions with it. No one institution has been so strongly interwoven into our national life as the National Church. For at least

---

[1] My revered friend Bishop Thirlwall seems to have claimed Jeremie Taylor as a ' Broad Churchman.' I always hesitate to express any dissent from the judgment of so great a man ; but it seems to me very clear indeed that Jeremie Taylor was only Broad because he was a many-sided man, and because in an intolerant age he pleaded for toleration. In the modern and technical sense of the word he was no more a ' Broad Churchman ' than Ussher was a Low Churchman. Ussher is supposed to have been a strong Calvinist, on the strength of his having written Ussher's Catechism. It is doubtful whether the book is his at all. If it be, it was a very early and crude production, and in his controversy with Rome he assumes the definite position of strict Anglicanism, or, as it is called, Anglo-Catholicism.

1,200 years the Church has been as much England as
the State has been. Notwithstanding the great changes
from the time of Augustine to the time of Anselm,
and then to the time of Cranmer, and still again to
our own time, yet no national institution has changed
so little as the Church. There was a time when England had no single Sovereign, when it had no true Parliament, when all the relations of noble to peasant,
governor to governed, man to man, were utterly unlike
what they are now; but the relation of the Church to
the people, amidst all corruptions and reforms, has
ever been substantially the same. I am certain that
you cannot rend the Church out of the national life
without shaking every other institution to its base. As
I am a loyal subject to my Sovereign, and as I believe
in the liberty of an English citizen, I do not wish to
see the English Church cease to be part of the English
Constitution. I am prepared, if Providence so orders
it, to accept a Republican Government and a Disestablished Church. I think the Church politically
would then be far stronger than it is now; but I do
not think the nation would be happier, I feel sure it
would not be so free, I fear it would be less religious.
The extreme schools who wish for all this would be
far less likely to find toleration for themselves when
they had had their will. I confidently expect, if I live
to see disestablishment, that I shall see, after some
throes and struggles, the Church settling down again
on its true basis as a reformed Catholic member of the
one great Body, its more sound and moderate adherents
being strong in the ascendant; but I know that it will
be obliged to entrench itself more firmly than hereto-
fore, and that therefore it must narrow its borders; that

so it will inevitably become more exclusive, throwing off the stragglers from either side. Thus those who are compassing the disestablishment of the Church are really working for their own exclusion from its pale.

Again, though the Church by disestablishment would probably become more exclusive, I do not see that it would be certainly more united. Its first danger would be utter disruption—a division into three distinct and discordant sects. If, as I should hope, it were to escape this, it would still contain within itself the elements which at present foster its divisions; and neither the American nor the Irish disestablished Church offer us a very encouraging picture of union. The same causes work amongst them that are at work amongst ourselves; and they produce the same results.

Lastly, whatever evils there may be in our parochial system, the good immensely overbalances the evil; and disestablishment would destroy all this. In the towns, perhaps, the parochial system is weak, but in our country villages the country clergyman forms a centre round which all gathers and circulates; a man of education, sympathising alike with rich and poor; in some instances almost the only civilising power in the place; with a modest independence that need not truckle to power, and which at the same time prevents him from merely courting popular favour. He may, no doubt, have some temptation to indolence and self-indulgence, and there are too many that yield to this; he may live in a narrow sphere and so may see but in a narrow circle; he may, in some cases, be wholly unfitted for his calling; but I doubt whether, on the whole, any Church or nation has ever produced a more moral, religious, honest, and conscientious body of men, lay or clerical,

than the English country clergymen at this time. Disestablishment would inevitably sweep all this away.
The town clergy would very likely be richer and,
perhaps, more efficient than they are at present; but
the resident, educated, often refined, country rector
would soon cease out of the land. It would not be
possible to provide endowments which would maintain
such men amongst us; and, unhappily, we know that
men must live if we want them to work. How country
villages and moorland hamlets could be Christianised,
when all this had passed away, no prophecy can tell. All
depends on it at the present time. Even the irregular
agency of Wesleyans and Dissenters holds on to it, like
ivy on an oak. Lop down the tree and you will lose
the verdure.

To recur once more to disruption and secession,
threatened so freely from the right hand and the
left; first of all, 'to whom shall we go?' I do not
believe that 'Evangelicals' are prepared to join any
sect of Dissenters, nor that 'Ritualists' are disposed to
submit themselves to Rome. The fate of Free Churches
is to weaken by secession the influence of their own
school, and to strengthen the opposite school, and then
gradually to fade away. A Free Church of England,
as a secession and as distinct from the great National
Church, is quite sure to fail. 'Our strength,' the
strength of both parties, 'is to sit still.' Fair tole-
rance of one for the other, and fair effort by lawful
persuasion and Christian argument to increase the
influence of our own convictions and sentiments; this
is the constitutional, the wise, and the successful way
of working in such a society as our own. Every other
brings mischief on that society, and mostly ruin on the

F

workers of mischief. We have plenty of enemies without, watching to widen the breach between us. Alas! that we should have to call fellow-Christians our enemies. But it is certain that Romanists, political Dissenters, and secularists of all sorts, are united, if in nothing else, at least in this—that they joy over our disunion, and that they lose no occasion for exaggerating its magnitude, and for trying to increase it. They, at least, all think that they can weaken us by destroying our national existence. I believe they are mistaken. I believe that England's Church is much deeper in England's heart than they suppose. Notwithstanding our divisions, notwithstanding our excesses, see how the people gather round us, crowd our churches, give freely of their wealth, give largely of their labour, which is more than wealth; see how even our communicants daily multiply where those who minister Communion give it freely and fully. Yes, wherever there is earnest zeal, even when there lacks much wisdom with the zeal, laymen always are to be found supporting and honouring their churches and their clergy; and, if once the Church was shaken off by the State, there can be no doubt that with still greater readiness and with more educated intelligence the nation would rise up in defence and for the maintenance of that ancient House which has been the home of Christian and loving hearts in England since first Christian faith and Christian hope were sown in the midst of it. I do not think Romanism or Nonconformity would gain by what they think would be our ruin. Infidelity and indifference would gain, not Christian Dissent of any type. But, surely, we ought not to play into their hands and help their tactics. Deeply do I sympathise, on the one hand, with that devoted love for the ancient traditions of the faith, with that warm attachment for the Catholic integrity of the Church's body, which is the watchword of one school amongst us. Deeply do I sympathise, on the other, with that love of purity in doctrine which is zealous for the honour of our Lord and King, refusing to permit any fellowship in His great redeeming labour either to Saints or to saintliness, to powers without or to powers within ourselves. True Catholic piety and true Evangelical purity are, I am very sure, compatible with each other. Only, let us look largely at both, not narrowly and exclusively on one alone. The Church, the Sacraments, the apostolic ministry, set forth, exalt, and enthrone Jesus Christ, sole Saviour, Head and King. There is none other name under heaven which the Church of God proclaims to the world as that by which it can be saved. Let us not rend the seamless coat, nor even cast lots on it whose it shall be. It is the one priceless heritage of Christians, and it is held as an undivided whole by the Church of Christ.

> I am, Reverend Brethren,
>> Your affectionate Brother and
>>> Chief Pastor in Christ,

>>>> E. H. WINTON.

FARNHAM CASTLE: *October* 1875.

LONDON : PRINTED BY
SPOTTISWOODE AND CO., NEW-STREET SQUARE
AND PARLIAMENT STREET

www.ingramcontent.com/pod-product-compliance
Lightning Source LLC
Chambersburg PA
CBHW022152090426
42742CB00010B/1490